STEGOSAURUS
AND OTHER PLAINS DINOSAURS

by **Dougal Dixon**

illustrated by
Steve Weston and **James Field**

PICTURE WINDOW BOOKS
Minneapolis, Minnesota

Picture Window Books
5115 Excelsior Boulevard
Suite 232
Minneapolis, MN 55416
877-845-8392
www.picturewindowbooks.com

Printed in the United States of America.

Library of Congress Cataloging-in-Publication Data
Dixon, Dougal.
Stegosaurus and other plains dinosaurs / written by
Dougal Dixon ; illustrations by James Field, Steve
Weston ; diagrams by Stefan Chabluk ; cover art by
Steve Weston.
p. cm. — (Dinosaur find)
Includes bibliographical references and index.
ISBN 1-4048-0668-7
1. Dinosaurs—Juvenile literature. 2. Grassland
animals—Juvenile literature. I. Field, James, 1959- ill.
II. Weston, Steve, ill. III. Chabluk, Stefan, ill. IV. Title.
QE861.5.D65 2005
567.9—dc22   2004007308

Acknowledgments
This book was produced for Picture Window Books by
Bender Richardson White, U.K.

Illustrations by James Field (pages 4–5, 7, 13,
15, 17) and Steve Weston (cover and pages 9,
11, 19, 21).
Diagrams by Stefan Chabluk.
All photographs copyright Digital Vision.

Consultant: John Stidworthy, Scientific Fellow of
the Zoological Society, London, and former
Lecturer in the Education Department, Natural
History Museum, London.

Reading Adviser: Rosemary G. Palmer, Ph.D.
Department of Literacy, College of Education,
Boise State University, Idaho.

Types of dinosaurs
In this book, a red shape at the top of a left-hand page shows the animal was a meat-eater. A green shape shows it was a plant-eater.

Just how big—or small— were they?
Dinosaurs were many different sizes. We have compared their size to one of the following:

 Chicken
2 feet (60 cm) tall
Weight 6 pounds (2.7 kg)

 Adult person
6 feet (1.8 m) tall
Weight 170 pounds (76.5 kg)

 Elephant
10 feet (3 m) tall
Weight 12,000 pounds
(5,400 kg)

TABLE OF CONTENTS

WHAT'S INSIDE?

Dinosaurs! These dinosaurs lived on the plains. Find out how they survived millions of years ago and what they have in common with today's animals.

LIFE ON THE PLAINS

Dinosaurs lived between 230 million and 65 million years ago. The world did not look the same then. The land and seas were not in the same places. Many dinosaurs lived on the plains. The plains were open country with a few ferns and trees. Some dinosaurs of the plains traveled in groups.

A pack of fierce meat-eating *Deinonychus* stalked the plains. They would only chase the big plant-eaters because the little ones were too fast.

ALLOSAURUS

Pronunciation:
AL-o-SAW-rus

Allosaurus waited for big herds of plant-eaters. Using their strong back legs, they ran across the plains to attack. They trapped a plant-eater away from its herd. The *Allosaurus* used their claws and sawlike teeth for killing.

Fighting today

Lions often fight over their prey like *Allosaurus* did millions of years ago.

Size Comparison

A pair of *Allosaurus* fought over a dead animal. One of them had killed it, and the other wanted to steal it.

7

APATOSAURUS

Apatosaurus ate leaves and twigs. Its long neck made the food easy to reach. It used its narrow, peglike teeth to rake the leaves off plants. *Apatosaurus* also swallowed stones to help grind up the plant food.

Long necks today

Giraffes have long necks. They can feed in high trees like *Apatosaurus* once did.

Size Comparison

8

An *Apatosaurus* lumbered across the wide plains, crushing the ferns. Its little eyes may have seen food miles away.

CARNOTAURUS
Pronunciation:
KAR-no-TOR-us

Carnotaurus had a short head with two dull horns. Its skin was covered in bumps and scales. It was the biggest meat-eater of its time. *Carnotaurus* traveled in herds and walked on its strong back legs. It had tiny arms.

Horns today

An African buffalo has horns on its head. It uses them in fights like *Carnotaurus* did.

Size Comparison

Carnotaurus would often head-butt each other. They would fight to see which one would lead the herd. They wouldn't get hurt. The loser would just back away.

DEINONYCHUS

Pronunciation:
dye-NON-I-kus

Deinonychus hunted in packs. They grabbed prey with their long fingers and slashed with their claws. They used the big claw on their feet for killing. *Deinonychus* stood on one foot and slashed with the other.

Noisy hunters today

Wolves hunt in packs and howl like *Deinonychus* did long ago.

Size Comparison

A pack of *Deinonychus* prowled the edge of the plains. They looked for other dinosaurs to attack.

13

GALLIMIMUS

Gallimimus was a lightweight dinosaur. It had long legs and ran a long way to get away from meat-eaters. The arms and fingers of a *Gallimimus* were weak. It had no teeth in its jaws, so it ate insects and fruit.

Fast feet today

Ostriches can run as fast as *Gallimimus* did. They run away from danger, too.

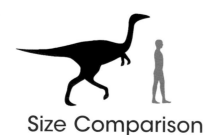

Size Comparison

A *Gallimimus* would run across the open plains. It could easily outrun the big dinosaurs.

15

HYPSILOPHODON

Pronunciation:
hip-see-LOAF-o-don

Hypsilophodon ate short or small plants like horsetails and ferns. It used its sharp, narrow beak to nip out the best shoots and leaves. *Hypsilophodon* ran quickly on its long legs and long toes. It also had a long tail.

Quick escape today

Gazelles eat short plants. They run away from enemies like *Hypsilophodon* did millions of years ago.

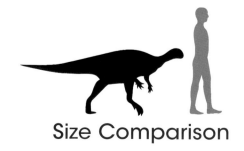

Size Comparison

Large meat-eaters often chased *Hypsilophodon*. *Hypsilophodon* would burst out of the bushes and run across the plains to escape.

SALTASAURUS

Pronunciation:
SAWL-tuh-SAW-rus

Saltasaurus was a slow-moving dinosaur. It was a huge, long-necked plant-eater. It raked leaves from trees with its peglike teeth. Its back was covered in armor. No meat-eater would attack this big, heavy dinosaur.

Raking leaves today

Moose are big, heavy plant-eaters that rake leaves from trees like *Saltasaurus* did.

Size Comparison

With its long neck, a *Saltasaurus* could feed on treetops. It would stand on its back legs to reach even higher.

STEGOSAURUS

Pronunciation:
STEG-o-SAW-rus

The plates on *Stegosaurus* might have been covered in skin. Wind blowing around them would have helped cool the dinosaur. The plates might have been brightly colored and used for signaling to others.

Cooling off today

An elephant has big ears that help cool its body like the plates on a *Stegosaurus* once did.

Size Comparison

A *Stegosaurus* moved along, nibbling the plants on the ground. It was a bright splash of color on the plains.

WHERE DID THEY GO?

Dinosaurs are extinct, which means that none of them are alive today. Scientists study rocks and fossils to find clues about what happened to dinosaurs.

People have different explanations about what happened. Some people think a huge asteroid that hit Earth caused all sorts of climate changes. This then caused the dinosaurs to die. Others think volcanic eruptions caused the climate to change and that killed the dinosaurs. No one knows for sure, though.

GLOSSARY

ferns—plants with finely divided leaves known as fronds; ferns are common in damp woods and along rivers

herds—large groups of animals that move, feed, and sleep together

horsetails—plants with tall, thin upright stems, sprays of green branches, and tiny leaves

insects—small, six-legged animals; they include ants, bees, beetles, and flies

packs—groups of animals that hunt and kill together

prey—animals that are hunted by other animals for food; the hunters are known as predators

rake—to strip off as if pulling with a comb or garden rake

signaling—making a sign, warning, or hint

Find Out More

At the Library

Clark, Neil, and William Lindsay. *1001 Facts About Dinosaurs.* New York: Backpack Books, Dorling Kindersley, 2002.

Dixon, Dougal. *Dougal Dixon's Amazing Dinosaurs.* Honesdale, Pa.: Boyds Mills Press, 2000.

Holtz, Thomas, and Michael Brett-Surman. *Dinosaur Field Guide.* New York: Random House, 2001.

On the Web

FactHound offers a safe, fun way to find Web sites related to this book. All of the sites on FactHound have been researched by our staff.
www.facthound.com

1. Visit the FactHound home page.

2. Enter a search word related to this book, or type in this special code: 1404806687.

3. Click on the Fetch It button.

Your trusty FactHound will fetch the best Web sites for you!

Index